ALL CORDOBA

Text, photographs, lay-out, reproduction, printing and binding, entirely designed and created by the Technical Department of F.I.S.A.

Rights of total or partial reproduction and translation reserved.

Copyright of this edition for photographs and text: © F.I.S.A., Industrias Gráficas.

1st edition, September 1972

editorial **escudo de oro, s.a.** Palaudarias, 26 - Barcelona, 4 - Spain

Impreso en España - Printed in Spain - Dep. Legal B. 47414-XV

An aspect of the façade of the Mosque, with the arches of its unmistakable gates evoked and projected on this beautiful picture of the XIX century.

A view of the Roman bridge over the Guadalquivir, between the Arabian ruins of the windmill of Albolafia.

FROM ROMAN CORDOVA TO THE SPLENDOUR OF THE CALIPHATE

History begins for Cordova with the Roman Conquest. Before, in prehistoric times, the Chelenses left a few remains of their nebulous passing through the lands of Cordova, and according to Estrabon, it was also visited by the Turdulos.

It is possible that the Phoenicians got as far as Cordova. A few of these seem to have enrolled in the Carthaginian armies, in the front line of which Hannibal marched against Rome...

There have been infinite hypothesis put forward about the origin of the word "Cordova". There are those who say it is derived from the Hebrew word *kortz* or the Phoenician word *kord*, that means *gold*, so that the ancient *Cordova* meant *place of gold*. For his part, Humboldt extracts the etimology of Cordova from *car* or *cor*, which means *height*, and *river*, that is "alto cerca del río" (high up on the river), an explanation that harmonizes perfectly with the location of the city on the banks of the Guadalquivir.

With the arrival of the Romans, Cordova began its historical steps, that centuries later, would result as being momentous not only for Spain, but also for nearly all the Mediterranean basin. Towards the year 169 B.C., Claudio Marcelo installed in Cordova a Roman colony. The city, converted into "Colonis Patricia", now had an illustrious name. Agripa, Julius Caesar, Pompey, Séneca and other great men seem to have attached themselves to Cordova. The Christian blood spilt by the martyrs San Acisclo and Santa Victoria, patron saints of the city, began to spiritually fertilize the Cordovan lands.

A panoramic view of Cordova, its hierarchy in the middle in the form of the large profile of the Mosque Cathedral and the Guadalquivir flowing in the foreground.

The characteristic rectangle of the Mosque certifies, over the topography of the city, the existence of a splendid historical past.

Puerta del Puente, with the Triunfo de San Rafael at the side, that gives access to the city across the Roman stone that rides over the Guadalquivir, guarded by the Calahorra.

MOSLEM CORDOVA

Cordova was conquested towards the end of the year 711 by the Arabian troops under the orders of Mugueiz El Rumi and, five years later, the Emir Al-Horr converted the city into the capital of moslem Spain. Until the middle of the VIII century Cordova was an Emirate, dependant on the Caliphate of Damasco, the history of which is presided over by a turbulent wake of political feuds, and bloody meetings between different Arabian tribes: Sirios, Medineses and Berberiscos.

In the year 756 the Omeya, Abderraman I, under whose Emirate construction of the mosque began, broke the ties of El-Andalus with Damasco and governed in Cordova as an independant Emir. In this epoch was begun a brilliant historical process that culminated in the X century with the foundation of the Caliphate of Cordova, a city that numbered in the times of Abderraman III no less than 500,000 inhabitants and some 3,000 mosques.

7

A partial view of the exterior the Mosque, that allows you to appreciate the size of its walls.

A beautiful view of the exterior of the Mosque-Cathedral, with the Virgen de los Faroles and the bell tower at the side.

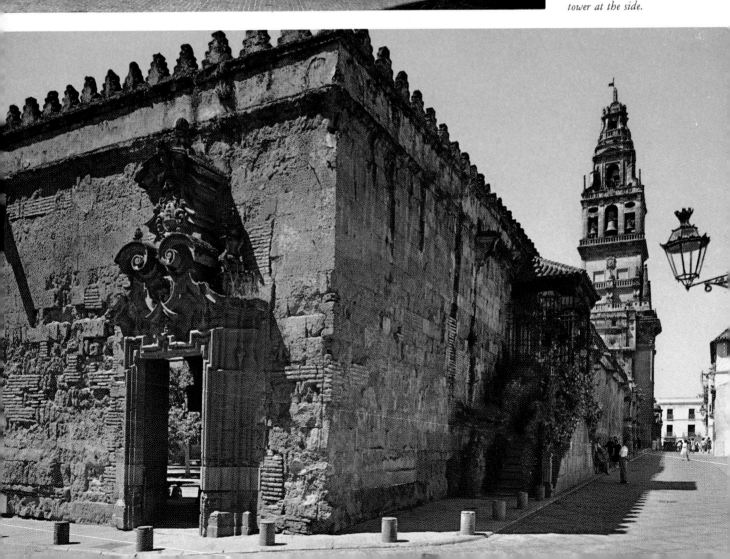

A brilliant aspect of the filigreed Puerta del Perdón, beautiful mudéjar style.

The Puerta del Perdón, situated in the northern part of the Mosque, constitutes the principal entrance to the temple.

The fountain of the olive in the Patio de los Naranjos, with the tower of the Cathedral in the background.

THE MOSQUE

The works were begun in the year 785, under the patronage of Abderraman I, the Emir who made moslem Spain independant. The mosque of Cordova, emblem and compendium of Spanish-Arabian art, was inaugurated in the year 793 by Hixem I. The unmistakable outline of the mosque is found in the same place, where it seems, there was a Visigothic Basilica dedicated to San Vicente by Recaredo after having renounced Arianism. It is the architectural symbol representing the grandeur of the Caliphate of Cordova. The mosque is something more than the work of a man or the historical or artistical summary of an epoch, it represents the will to survive of a whole race of people.

In the architecture of the mosque one can observe four autonomous styles, representing four different epochs. The first epoch dates from the year 785 to the year 793. The temple was in those days a perfect square. The main door faced north and led onto a patio in which were placed eleven airy arches that joined up with the eleven naves of the central part. Abderraman II iniciated the second epoch of the mosque (833-848), that extended the building to the south and added another nine arches.

With Al-Haquem II was begun the most brilliant epoch of the mosque, that when newly lengthened towards the south, acquired, between 964 and 965, the shape of a gigantic rectangle.

The marvellous frontal arch of the Mihrab exhibits fascinating colouring.

A lateral view of the Mihrab, in which you can appreciate the elegance of the columns on which it sits.

In this epoch eleven arches were opened in the exterior wall of the temple, the naves were enlarged, adding to them thirteen columns in a line, and the famous Mihrab was constructed, the decoration of which is now considered to be the most important work of the Byzantine art in Spain. It is the star moment for the mosque of Cordova. The temple has been converted spiritually into the authentic enlightenment of the moslem faith, and its walls are like burning embers anointed by the arts. One can understand perfectly how dazzled was the poet who praises its greatness: *The gold shines in your ceilings like the lightning that crosses the clouds.*

The fourth epoch of the mosque began in the year 987. Almanzor was the one who inspired it. The extension of the temple was made this time towards the east. Several more arches were opened and eight more naves were constructed. Although later numerous reforms were made to the mosque of Cordova.

An aspect of the beautiful byzantine mosaic which shows off the capitals of the columns that support the horseshoe-shaped arch of the Mihrab.

The dome of
the Mihrab
shows off a
fascinating
coloured
mosaic.

A beautiful
close up of the
incomparable
mosaic of the
chapel of
the Mihrab.

A magical framing of the Capilla Real, of pure Mudéjar style.

One arrives at the mosque from the centre of the city, going down any side street, all surprisingly clean and quite steep.

On entering the mosque the first impression you get is a little strange: One feels invaded by a sort of mixture of alarm and disorientation. The sensation of psychic uneasiness lasts until you have been able to digest, at least to a certain point, the cultural Spanish-Moslem synthesis that is projected, overflowing in the atmosphere of the temple.

It is necessary to give a daring jump backwards, towards the historical past and try to understand, between the events in time, the splendid light that illuminates the epoch of the Caliphate of Cordova.

An impressing aspect of the Mihrab and the naves of Alhaken II.

Only in this way is it possible to walk with a minimum of equilibrium under the arches of the mosque, that continue one after another, persistently, in a fantastic architectural sum, that seems to imitate the infinite.

The Arabesque works that keep passing in front of the eyes reclaim a lingering look, are of the finest of first class art. However, the mosque of Cordova is, or at least, it seems to be, less delicate than the Alhambra of Granada. It is natural: the first was constructed more for death and the second more for life. The mosque makes the spirit concentrate, as much as the Alhambra makes it forget everything.

The main door of the mosque faces the north, it is called the "Puerta del Perdón". It was constructed in the XIV century and is a beautiful example of Moslem architecture. On this side is found the airy tower constructed by Hernán Ruiz, that is crowned by a San Rafael carved by Pedro de Paz, that opens the door of the "Caño Gordo", at the side of the exterior altar where the "Virgen de los Faroles" is found.

The temple accedes, through the western wall, by the "Postigo de la leche", which is ogival style, the denomination of which comes from the fact that in other epochs orphanned children were put there to be taken in by the clergy. Another entrance from this section is the "Puerta de los Deanes", that, the same as the "Postigo de la leche", joins up with the "Patio de los Naranjos". Very near is the artistic "Puerta de San Esteban", joined to the ancient wall of the temple, that of "San Miguel", with ogival decorations of the XVI century, and the "Postigo del Palacio or de la

A flaming print of the principal nave, with the Mihrab in the background.

A beautiful perspective of the Mihrab through the columns that make a guard of honour at its entrance.

A partial view of the impressing maze of columns.

A beautiful view that lets one appreciate the beauty of the columns and capitals of the naves constructed by Almanzor.

The oriental presence of the aqueducts of the chapel of the Lucernario impregnated with artistic majesty.

Under the hieratic arches of the Mosque the throbbing heartbeat of the Caliphate of Cordova seems to introduce itself even more.

The arches and columns give the Mosque an air of mysterious oriental solemnity.

Paloma", that shows off Gothic additions of the XV century, and on the sides of which open out two doors of pure Arabian style. While in the Southern wall, that goes along the bank of the Guadalquivir, there is no door; on the eastern side you can admire the "Postigo del Sagrario", the door that gives access to the Christian Cathedral, and several doors opened by Almanzor in the last architectural stage of the mosque of Moslem inspiration.

From the exterior, more than a temple the Mosque-Cathedral looks like a military fortress.

If you enter the Mosque by the "Puerta del Perdón", or by the "Postigo de la leche", or the "Puerta de los Deanes", you will be surprised by the greenness, totally unexpected, with palm trees and cypresses entering into the poetical atmosphere of the "Patio de los Naranjos".

A little later, almost without moving, already inside the Mosque, the maze like presence of the colums engraves itself, along the length and breadth of the spacious naves, the stamp of the overflowing oriental fantasy intoxicated by the religious rigour. Dominating the first gust of amazement, from all sides the senses receive constant calls: from the capitals, ionic, corinthian or mixed or from

The importance of the amplification done on the Mosque by Almanzor is perfectly reflected in the architectural grandeur of the naves supportted by the so called Laberinto (maze) of columns.

the artistic panelling that shows off magnificent polichromed carvings, from the historical aqueducts, or from the very hieratic columns... Everything seems to keep in its groin the great mystery of an esoterical past. Our capacity of admiration will experiment a sensation like that of impotency when looking at this dazzling Arabian marvel that occupies a priviledged place in the mosque: el Mihrab. The richness of the three chapels which form it, are really like a fairy-tale. The greatness of the vaults that wear byzantine mosaics of surprising beauty, the marble soberly worked, the large multicoloured columns and the golden capitals, dazzle and amaze us.

The "Mihrab" is one of the highest peaks of the Arabian architecture in Spain. Here all the pomp and oriental fantasy have been capsized, here, where in times of the Caliphate the valuable Koran was guarded, topped with pearls and rubies, copied by the Caliph Oman and authenticated by his own blood.

The perfect geometry of the arches and columns of the Laberinto seem to transmit an enigmatic message from the past.

The naves of Almanzor support the back of the Altar Mayor of the Cathedral, architecturally joining two conceptions of different worlds.

*An aspect of
the primitive
part of the
Mosque.*

A partial view of the dome of the Capilla de Villaviciosa.

THE CATHEDRAL

After the city of Cordova was conquested by Fernando III in the year 1236, the Mosque was converted into a Cathedral. After the transformations that were necessary to be able to adapt the church to the necessities of the Catholic cult, the Capilla Mayor was constructed in the times of the Catholic Kings.

On the dome of the Mihrab one can admire this enormous shell made with only one stone.

A beautiful crucifix that presides over the façade of the Capilla de Villaviciosa.

A magnificent perspective of the choir and crossing of naves in the Cathedral.

The modifications brought about on the ancient Mosque were done in a sensible way, in the northern zone, where all the naves were closed, except that which, with the name of "Puerta de las Palmas", came to be the entrance to the Cathedral. There were also built fifty two chapels and the sumptuous Mihrab was converted into the vestry of the actual chapel of San Pedro. The transformation of Mosque to Cathedral took 243 years (1523-1766).

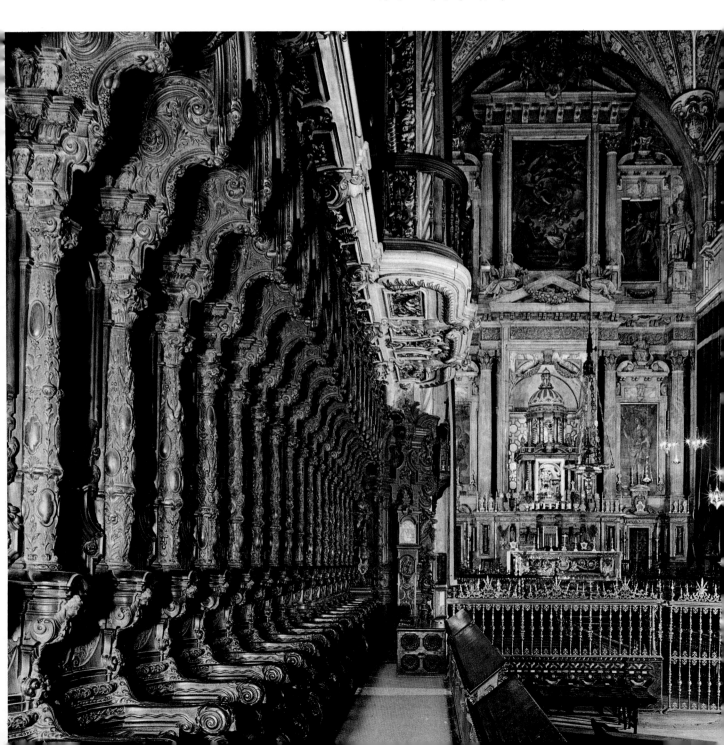

The Christian altars are, under the Arabian arches, frankly surprising, and one has to make a great effort to be able to understand, within the historical bounds of art its architectural conjunction.

Powerfully calling one's attention, inside the ambit of the Cathedral, the already mentioned Capilla Mayor, with its valuable jasper and marble altar piece and its marble Baroque tabernacle, the Churrigueresque pulpits that shelter under the Arabian horse-shoe shaped arches where the naves cross and the magnificent seats of the choir, carved in mahogany by Duque Cornejo in the XVIII century, is an admirable sample of Baroque art. In the Chapel of San Bartolomé, where Luis de Góngora is buried, the fustian shadow of Polifemo comes into the path of one's imagination, and in that of the Animas, the last resting place of Inca Garcilaso de la Vega, the millenary shadow of the Pre-Columbus America seems to be projected; while in the Chapel of the Concepción one stops to admire some splendid carvings by Pedro de Mena and in that of the Cardenal Salazar, one can see the spulture of Santa Teresa sculptured by José de Mora. And still there is the rich treasure of the Cathedral to be seen, where the beautiful Monstrance is kept, the principal work of art of Enrique de Arfe, that was taken out in a procession for the first time the day of Corpus Christi in 1518.

The heraldry of Castilla and León excels itself, certifying the stubborn Christian victory, in the crypt of the Capilla Real.

A majestic aspect of the nave of the Cathedral, with the Capilla Mayor in the background.

Medallion of the New Testament, carved in wood, that adorns the seats of the choir.

*A view of the
pulpit of
the Evangelio.*

A beautiful perspective of the walls,
with the monument to Averroes
in the foreground.

THE RAMPARTS

Cordova was already surrounded by walls in the Roman epoch. Posteriorly, the Arabs built their own walls making use of the remains of the Roman ones in many places.

One can still contemplate two gates of the numerous ones that existed in the past: The "Puerta de Sevilla", constructed originally in the X century, and that of Almodovar, the airy horseshoe-shaped arch guarded by two gallant keeps. Also still standing the Renaissance "Puerta del Puente".

An evoking corner of the Moorish
patio, with the Torre de los Leones
in the background, in the Alcázar
of the Catholic Kings.

The statue of the Cordovan poet
Ibn Hazm, who wrote El Collar de
la paloma. Tratado sobre el amor
y los amantes, is found on the
beautiful arches of the Puerta de
Sevilla.

THE ALCAZAR, PALACE-FORTRESS, OF THE CHRISTIAN KINGS

The building was begun in the year 1328, under the patronage of Alfonso XI. In this "Alcázar" the Catholic king and queen lived while they were waging war in the field during the conquest of Granada.

It is of Mudéjar style and it takes the shape of a square. On the corners of the construction there are keeps and they are sourrounded by beautiful gardens.

Still standing, overlooking the countryside that surrounds the Alcázar, are three of its towers: that of the Río, that of the Homenaje, in which there is a splendid hall with Gothic capitals, and that of Los Leones, of Mudéjar design.

In the Alcázar are conserved different allusive archaelogical remains of the past history of Cordova, among those that stand out is a marble tomb, from the II to III century, and seven magnificent Roman mosaics. Also of great interest are the ancient baths, the delicious Mudéjar patio and the marvellous gardens.

History has taken root and stopped many times in the Alcázar of Cordova. Here, Boabdil el Chico lived as a prisoner, last monarch of Moslem Granada; here the Catholic Kings received Christopher Columbus before he started out on his first journey to the New World. And, from 1490-1821, the Inquisition was housed in the Alcázar.

A poetical close up of the gardens and pond of the Alcázar of the Catholic Kings.

A suggestive aspect of the swimming pools and gardens of the Alcázar.

A beautiful perspective of the ponds and gardens of the Alcázar, in harmonic hierarchy with the green of the myrtle, the palms and the cypresses.

The Gate and the monument of Alfonso X el Sabio give this charming corner the category of a historical milestone.

THE SYNAGOGUE

It was constructed in the year 1314. It is a square one storey building and is entered by crossing a small courtyard with a porch of columns and a gate at the right hand side. It is situated approximately in the middle of the calle de los Judíos, not far from the Plaza de Maimónides, where the Municipal museum of Cordovan Art and Bullfighting is.

The synagogue was a Hebrew temple until 1492, the year in which the Catholic Kings decreed the expulsion of the Jews. Later a hospital for people with hidrophobia was installed within it, being put under the appellation of San Crispín, the patron saint of shoemakers, who installed their cofradia in the synagogue.

In the small room you can admire the Mudéjar plaster work that decorates its walls and beautiful balconies, on the arches of which are found writings of the Psalms. On the bracket over which the ogival arch leans on one of the walls, the one on the western side, there is the following inscription, written in Arabian letters:

A Jehova, todo reino y poderío.

The synagogue of Cordova is the only one that exists in Andalusia and forms, with the two of Toledo, the only three Jewish temples that still exist today in Spain. It is a monument of great historical and artistic value.

Séneca seems to represent symbolically, from the pedestal of his statue and from the edge of the Puerta de Almodóvar, the spirit of Cordova.

At the entrance of the calle de los Judíos, is found, surrounded by flowers, the beautiful monument to Maimónides, the great Jewish thinker of Cordova.

An aspect of the interior of the Synagogue of Cordova, one of the only three Hebrew monuments of this sort, the othersare in Toledo that exist in Spain.

The door of access to the interesting Municipal Museum of Cordovan and Bullfighting Arts, installed in the beautiful building in which Maimónides lived.

PLAZUELA
DE
MAIMONIDES

THE JUDERIA

It concerns a district of great architectural personality. One can enter the Judería by the Puerta de Almodóvar, ancient Puerta de los Judíos. The first street that there is to the right is that of the Judíos, a zigzaging artery of a neat and absorbing district, propitious for the evocation. The Judería is formed by a complicated maze of small streets of a narrow and long outline. Nearly all of them come out into a small square of singular structure. That of the Judíos ends in the Plaza de Maimónides, the illustrious Jewish thinker, author of the "Guide of the perplexes".

An aspect of the beautiful patio in the picturesque Zoco of Cordova.

The entrance to the intimate sanctuary of San Bartolomé constitutes as a synthesis of the characteristical balanced architecture of Cordova.

THE CITY

The idiosyncrasy of the people of Cordova is founded on two fundemental pillars: The quiet roman classicism and the overflowing oriental fantasy of the Arabs, filled with passion and indolence. Through the two co-ordinations, the western and classical, and the Mohammedad and romantic, the singular character of the people of Cordova is found, whose principle features are elegant discretion and great friendliness. Very few peoples can boast of possesing such a natural distinction and outstanding personality as the people of Cordova

García Lorca said that Cordova is "the most melancholy city of Andalusia". And added:

> Pero Córdoba no tiembla,
> bajo el misterio confuso,
> pues si la sombra levanta
> en arquitectura el humo,
> un pie de mármol afirma
> su casto fulgor enjuto.

All the city is full of interesting monuments and its topography is literally invaded by the most noble and different architectural styles. To walk through Cordova means feasting the eyes and the senses on an incessant esthetic surprise. In any of its tiny streets, in any of its small squares, in the most forgotten corner, it is present, and miraculously alive, the cordovan spirit living to transmit through the ways of history and always eager for new artistical experiences.

An aerial view of the popular Plaza de la Corredera, where in the past bullfights and other spectacles were celebrated.

The presence of the vegetation shows up artistically against the whitewashed houses, making the Plaza de las Flores a paradise-like corner.

The gay colours of the beautiful Callejón de las Flores conjugates intimately with the immaculate cleanliness and the perfume that impregnates the air.

The Plaza de José Antonio presided over by the equestrian statue of the Gran Capitán and popularily known by the name of Plaza de Las Tendillas, is the urban centre of the modern Cordova. It is the heart of the cordial night life of Cordova, that expands through a few of the nearby streets, of modern structure, intensely humanized by the amiable presence of the wines of Montilla or of Moriles. From the top of one of the buildings that borders the Plaza de José Antonio, a clock lets one know of the tragic passing of time by striking the quarters of the hour with carillon and immediately afterwards a flamenco tune. A feature of the profound humour and good taste, so typical of the people of Cordova.

The Mosque is not far from the Plaza de José Antonio. It is only necessary to enter the street of Jesús María and immediately you will arrive at the Mosque to the left, also very near, are the museums, and to the right the Judería.

Everything in Cordova is edged with an authentic humane sense. After leaving the Plaza de José Antonio, going in any direction, you will find beautiful squares full of greenery and nearly always in flower, with a monument in the middle erected in the honour of some personage of Cordova: Arab, Jew or Christian.

If the Plaza de José Antonio is the most modern and dynamic of Cordova, that of the Corredera is the most popular and picturesque. It is porched, and resembles a little the Plaza Mayor in Madrid. It is a square which is full of vitality, with stalls, stands selling churros, the sale of material, clothes, shoes. All in the open air. Under the arches there are numerous bars and many gypsy like people, of these García Lorca said of their profile that it was:

*Viva moneda que nunca
se volverá a repetir.*

A flowery profile of the pretty calle de los Vinagreros.

The bust of Manolete, one of the great bullfighters of Cordova, is framed by flowers and palm trees.

The statue of the bishop Osio is found, hidden by a pair of elegant palm trees, in the charming Plaza de los Capuchinos.

It would be a never ending tale to say things about all the interesting spots that there are up and down the city. The character of the people of Cordova that comes across our path if we enter into the small street of Pedro Jiménez, that of Junio Gallon or the beautiful street of San Fernando. And the same way if we enter the flowery little street of Los Vinagreros or if we sit in the shade of the palm trees that surround the statue of the bishop Osio, Counsellor to Constantine the Great, in the Plaza de los Capuchinos.

A beautiful and flowery corner typical of Cordova.

The realism of the carving of the popular Cristo de los Faroles gives the precinct of the Plaza de los Dolores an air of emotional religion.

In the modern zone of the city standing out because of their spaciousness and vitality are the Avenues of Conde de Vallero, of América, of the Generalísimo, of Cervantes, of the Gran Capitán and of the Aeropuerto, that crosses the Gran Vía Park. The urban structure of the Cordova of today is modernly balanced and attractive. The harmony between the ancient and new does not break up the urban unity, as happens, unfortunately, in many other cities. García Lorca is the author of these verses:

> ¡Sevilla para herir!
> ¡Córdoba para morir!

Cordova is certainly a good place to die in, but without any doubt, it is also a good place to live in. The great poet Ibn Hazm, an arab from Cordova, seems to have known it by intuition, and at the same time enjoyed himself when writing in his beautiful work, *El collar de la Paloma,* some verses that sum up a delicate sensuality:

Reían las flores, y sus brazaletes mo-
vían al cobijo de una sombra difusa.
Los pajarillos nos ofrecen su más bella
[canción.
Unos endechaban su pena; otros gor-
[jeaban.
Corría libremente el agua entre no-
[sotros.
Ojos y manos podían lograr cuanto
[apetecían.

A suggestive nocturnal aspect of the dynamic Plaza de José Antonio, heart of the modern Cordova.

Under its potent modernity, Cordova conserves its genuine character intact, half Roman and half Arab, and its predisposition to integrate harmonously tradition and newness. A demonstration of this can be seen in the happy human spectacle that these beautiful girls of the Urban Police-force of Cordova make, whose gentle feminity does not stop them giving fines to the drivers who infringe the traffic laws...

Cordova is a beautiful open poem, that time goes on perfecting and beautifying without stopping. Art and life go arm in arm through the streets of Cordova. Nothing dies forever in Cordova, not even the past, that sleeps to be awoken in any moment, at the conspiracy of a monument or conciliating its evocation by the magic of a verse or the simple movement of the waters of the Guadalquivir.

In the streets of Cordova the driver finds to his pleasant surprise that the traffic is directed in many parts by beautiful young ladies.

Two gentle feminine members of the Municipal Police force of Cordova chatting in front of the statue of the Gran Capitán in the central Plaza de José Antonio.

The equestrian statue of the Gran Capitán presides, sung to by the murmur of the water from the fountains which surround it, over the civic dynamism of the Plaza de José Antonio.

An impressing modern façade of the Hotel Melia engraves on the urban profile of the city an air of throbbing vitality.

THE PATIOS OF CORDOVA

The charming patios of Cordova constitute one of the biggest attractions of the city. There are patios which are sometimes noble and other times profoundly popular, but always original and immaculately clean, neat, sweet smelling and full of plants and flowers.

Like everything in Cordova they constitute an authentic legacy from the historical past, the patios have two roots: the Roman and the Arabian. It seems, it was under the Roman rule when the patios of Cordova received great popularity.

A delicious corner of an ancient patio in Cordova.

The flower pots, the whitewashed well, the dionysiac vine leaves, the small cage and elemental ornaments, which, conjugated with simplicity and naturalism, made this beautiful patio of number 50, calle Basilio, take the prize of honour of the Festival of the patios of Cordova 1967, a charming corner with authentic popular flavour.

The patios of Cordova communicate directly with the rooms and galleries of the houses. Sometimes the communication between the patio and the interior of the building is established through windows and balconies and other times through gracious porch ways or through the railings that border the small roofs. The walls of the patio are literally invaded with flowers and climbing plants. Orange trees, lemon trees, flowers of a all kinds, flowers everywhere, perfume the atmosphere of the patio, they lend a polichromed air of continuous festival and create a miracle of calmness under the green shade in the middle of the city.

The patio invites one to rest, and to collect one's thoughts.

The colouring of a patio in Cordova constitutes an authentic gala

The good taste and the balanced ornamentation show up at first sight in this attractive patio of number 16, calle Cardenal Herrero.

The white arches that open out onto the small roof give a nice and humane note to the intense vegetation that invades the personal precinct of this delicious patio of number 15, calle Badanas, that obtained in 1967 the first prize of the patios of Cordova.

of colours. Only the white of the walls stands out alone or the gold of the lemons, the blood red of the carnations, the green of the leaves. For an artist in love with colour, a Cordovan patio would surely represent a powerful temptation: that of recreating plastically this atmosphere between beauty and godliness, profound and completely human. In spite of the Arabian taste for protecting and surrounding themselves in an esoteric family life, the course of which has a definite importance on the Cordovan patio; it still continued conserving the open structure of its Roman origin. The Renaissance influence was in this sense of considerable importance and contributed to the fact that the outlines of the patios were kept quite faithful to their origin. The railed gates, of magnificent wrought iron, allows you to see through them below to what was and is an immense flowery world of the patios of Cordova.

Apart from the exhuberant vegetation that literally invades all the space in a patio in Cordova, this also offers to the eyes, well balanced ornaments, the presence of murmuring fountains, poetical jets of water, beautiful pieces of ceramic, artistic iron work, gracious porches, elegant tiles and the bright whiteness of the walls, that here seem to be made of an all powerful plastic, mixing colours and joining angles.

The symphony of colours plays subtly, and tops, without announcing it, the angles of this beautiful patio in Cordova.

Through the artistic railings one sees perfectly the luminous intimacy of this elegant patio in Cordova.

You must not think that the Patio in Cordova is only present in the large mansions. It is also present in the most humble houses and its foundation, apart from of course the architectural distances of space and luxury, is the same in a palace as in a modest home. The patio of the most humble house in Cordova is a millionaire in flowers and in its precinct are found shade, water, and whiteness giving an air of hierarchy to the atmosphere and shunning in an insensible but pushing way all the risks of being humbled. The popular patios are like small enchanting gardens that, situated in the middle of the house, flood it with happiness and free beauty.

The personality of this patio of Cordova sits on the aristocratic harmony with which have been assembled the architectural and ornamental elements that integrate it.

So rooted is the patio and its significance in the life of the people of Cordova, that, also, celebrated every year, in the first fortnight in May, is the nice colourful Festival of the Patios of Cordova. All the people decorate their patios during this fortnight and compete to win the first prize.

A subtle air of gaiety and exotic feeling gives this gracious patio in Cordova an attractive and accused personality.

The ornamental sobriety and the pure taste stands out in the profile of this patio in Cordova in the calle los Rodríguez.

These spring festivals have a great importance in the rich Cordovan folklore. They begin in the patio, and flow out into the street. The squares are garlanded with beautiful crosses of May flowers, and the popular mood takes its course from the most varied folkloric colours inherited from a rich communicative past. The districts rival each other in the decoration of their patios and organize gay parties, that, celebrated intimately at first, soon extend to the streets and squares. The feet mark out the steps of a dance and from the throat comes a popular tune of a "soleá", full of feeling.

A whole world of evocations seems to be present in the porch of the patio de la Casa Obispal.

A delicious vegetal apotheosis joyfully invades the atmosphere of the patio de las rejas, one of the most beautiful of the Palacio de Viana.

*An attractive aspect of the
marvellous principal patio of
the Palacio del Marqués de Viana.*

*A beautiful corner of the patio
of the cancela, in the Palace del
Marqués de Viana.*

While the festival of the patios lasts, there are celebrated in Cordova, in the gardens of the Alcázar of the Christian Kings, in the square of the Plaza de la Corredera or in any other appropriate place, interesting recitals of flamenco songs, concerts of classical music, plays, dancing shows, song competitions of "cante jondo"

Many are the different types of patios that can be admired in Cordova. All have their interesting points and an accused personality. But perhaps it wouldn't be unjust to point out the fourteen patios of the Palace of the Marqués de Viana, an ancient house of the Villaseca family. The patio at the entrance is of the XVII century and is beautifully adorned, in the same way as the others, in which there are plenty of orange trees, cypresses, fountains, flowers. As a whole it is really like a paradise.

Other patios of particular beauty and personality are, that of the Casa Obispal; in the calle (street) Basilio, number 50; that of 16, calle Cardenal Herrero; that of 15, calle Badanas; one that is in the calle José Rey; another, in the calle de Don Rodrigo; that of 25, calle de Enmedio which has brick arches, a rustic kitchen and a well; that of number 29 of the same street, that boasts a porch of three white washed arches...

Everything is conjugated with difficult simplicity, unrepeatable workmanship of the work of art, in the atmosphere of this beautiful patio of the Palace of the Marqués de Viana, Cordovan by antonomasia.

An evoking view of the artistic gate of the church of the Magdalena, with the bell tower in the front part of the photo.

The monument to the bullfighter Manolete is found in front of the principal façade of the church of Santa Marina.

CHRISTIAN TEMPLES

Having conquested Cordova Fernando III el Santo founded in the city fourteen parishes. The corresponding temples or churches were constructed between the end of the XIII century and the beginning of the XIV century, and in their architectural lines one can see Romanesque, Gothic and Mudéjar elements, with Baroque additions incorporated in the XVII and XVIII centuries.

Among the Christian temples of notable artistic beauty, generally of one floor with three naves and polygonal presbiteries, stand out San Nicolás de la Villa, La Magdalena, Santa Marina, San Lorenzo and San Andrés.

San Nicolás de la Villa offers the individuality, within the group of churches dating back to the epoch

of the Reconquest, that it is made up of four square presbiteries. Its octagonal tower, that boasts a beautiful Mudéjar frieze and embattlements with flor de lis, is the most personal of the city.

The church of Santa Marina, in front of the façade of which is found the monument to Manolete, offers its ample air of a fortress and consists of three porches with smoothly pointed arches and a beautiful large rosette on the frontispiece.

The parish church of San Lorenzo has a large porch of the XIV century guarding its principal porchway, and riding over the arches, an elegant large rosette framed by half a dozen mouldings.

The temple of San Andrés is housed in the ancient district of silk embroiderers, where the basilica was erected under Arab rule in honour of San Zoilo. The actual church was built in the XVIII century and the only remaining parts of the temple constructed in the epoch of the Reconquest are the Ogival vault and the central vault, today converted into Sacrarium. Other temples of interest are the church of San Pedro, anterior basilica of the Moslem conquest reconstructed in the XVI century, the church of San Francisco, with a Greek-Romanesque porch and the inside of Churrigueresque style, and the chapel of San Bartolomé, of Gothic style with Mudéjar additions.

A magnificent close up of the church of San Lorenzo, in which you can appreciate the grace of the porch and the marvellous rosette.

A magnificent carving of Nuestra Señora de los Dolores.

The impressing image of el Cristo del Remedio de Animas, taken out in the procession through the streets of Cordova, on Easter Monday.

The processions continue, past the Mosque-Cathedral and through the winding and humanized surrounding streets. Among the statues taken out in the processions, stand out that of Nuestra Señora de los Dolores, Patron Saint of Cordova, that of Cristo de Remedio de Animas, that of the Rescatado and that of the Cristo de la Misericordia...

An artistic statue of the Virgin, who, on her luxurious shrine is taken out into the procession in the course of the celebrations of Easter Week in Cordova.

THE PLAZA DEL POTRO

Already famous in the lifetime of Cervantes, which he mentions in the pages of the *Quijote* and in *Rinconete y Cortadillo,* the Plaza (square) del Potro reached its highest popularity in the XVI and XVII centuries, when on its esplanade free and easy people congregated, types that lived on the edge of adventure, merchants with good noses for business and Spaniards without fortune waiting to be contracted for any kind of work.

On one side is the celebrated "Posa'da del Potro", in the centre, an airy stone fountain of the XVI century, crowned by a lively rearing foal, and on the other side is the façade of the ancient Hospital de la Caridad, constructed in the XV century, and the entrance to the Museums Provincial de Bellas Artes and of Romero de Torres. At one end of the square there is a monument erected in honour of San Rafael, and at the bottom, in the opposite direction, a view opens out to the lands of Cordova.

An aspect of the magnificent central room on the top floor of the Museo Provincial de Bellas Artes of Cordova.

A partial view of the Plaza del Potro, with its artistic fountain, constructed in 1577, in the foreground, and the façade of the ancient Hospital of the Caridad where the Museo Provincial de Bellas Artes is, in the background.

The magnificent Retable of the
Flagelación, work of art by Alfonso
de Aguilar, that you can admire
in the Museo Provincial de Bellas
Artes of Cordova.

A beautiful portrait of a friar, by
Zurbarán, that is kept in the
Museo Provincial of Cordova.

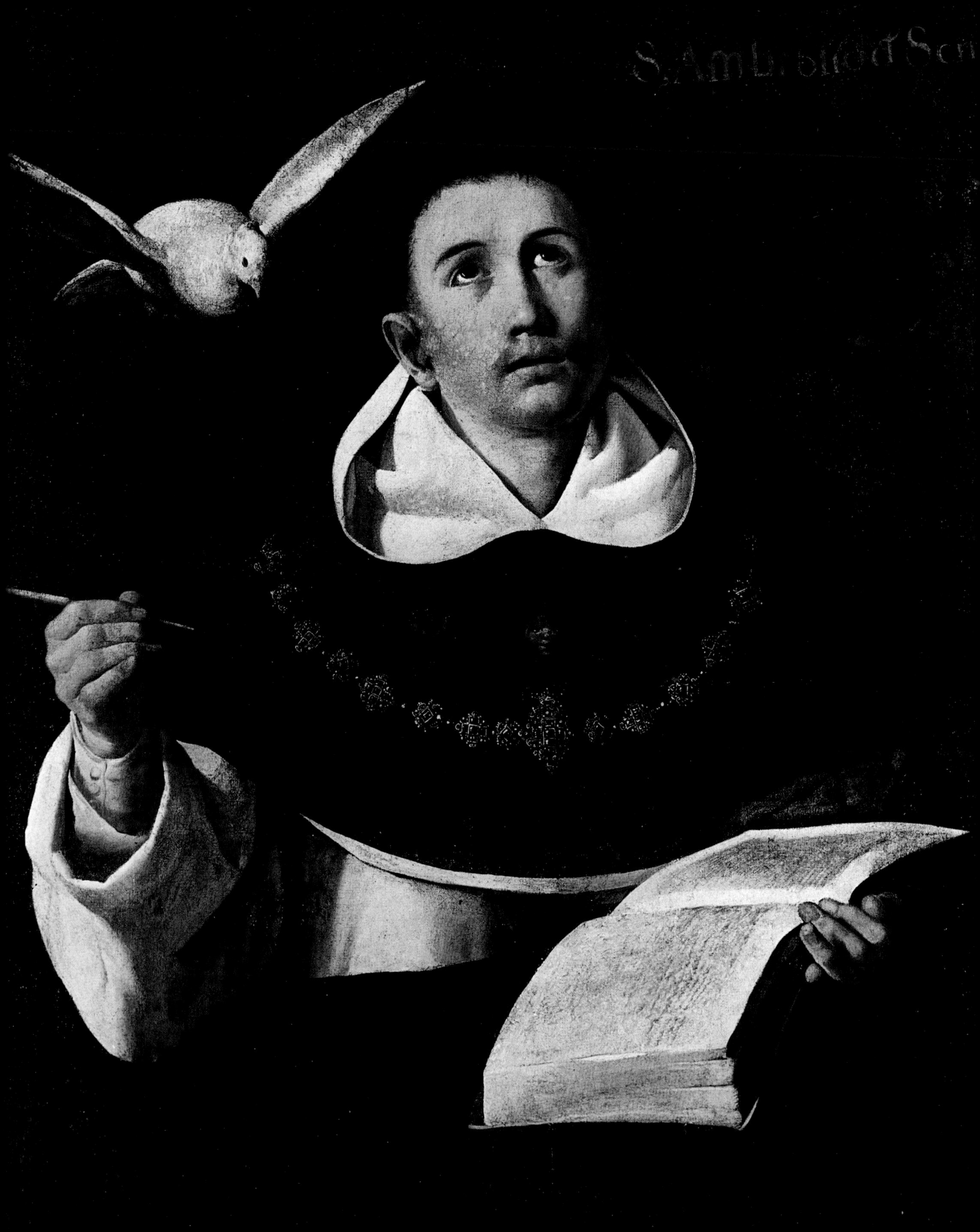

An aspect of the Living room-Studio of Romero de Torres.

The genius of Goya is shown in this magnificent portrait of "María Luisa", one of the most valuable pictures of the Museum of Cordova.

THE MUSEO PROVINCIAL DE BELLAS ARTES

This is situated in the Plaza del Potro, in the building that was the Hospital of the Santa Caridad de Nuestro Señor Jesucristo. A pretty garden, full of sculptures, is also the Antechamber of the Museum.

In the different rooms you can admire works by Alonso de Aguilar, Pedro Romana, Valdés Leal, Zurbarán, Bocanegra, Alonso Cano, Murillo, Ribera, Antonio del Castillo, Eugenio Lucas, Mengs, Goya...

Among the modern artists stand out works by Solana, Chicharro and Benedito...

There is a room of prints with works by Esteve Botey, Castro Gil, Pellicer and others.

The Museum also has an excellent collection of etchings by Ricardo Baroja and a room dedicated to the sculptor of Cordova, Mateo Inurria.

THE MUSEUM
JULIO ROMERO DE TORRES

This is installed in the same building as the Museo Provincial de Bellas Artes, on the other side of the garden, entering to the right. In one of the rooms you can contemplate the plans of the monument to Romero de Torres, work of Juan Cristóbal. In the different rooms of the museum are exhibited numerous pictures of this painter of Cordova, such as "La chiquita piconera", "Ofrenda al arte del toreo", "El poema de Córdoba", "Naranjas y Limones", "La Magdalena" and others.

The work by Romero de Torres, painter of the bronze skin, of the gypsies, and of passionate love Spanish-style, is perfectly represented here. Through all the museum flutters his plastic personal song to the women of Cordova, in the style of which Romero de Torres obtained a blending of colours difficult to better.

There is the painting of Romero de Torres, eminently literary, a clear mystification of women, that tuns the torrent of love for courses of tragic sensuality. To help you to interpret many of the pictures of this popular artist of Cordova, there is nothing more appropriate than to read the poem by García Lorca titled "Puñal".

"La chiquita piconera", famous work by Romero de Torres. ▷

"Ofrenda al arte del toreo", one of the most characteristical canvases of Romero de Torres, that can be contemplated in the pavilion of the Museo Provincial de Bellas Artes which is dedicated to this popular painter of Cordova.

THE ARCHAEOLOGICAL MUSEUM

It is situated in the Plaza de Jerónimo Páez, and is a beautiful building with an italian-style portal. One arrives at the museum having crossed a splendid patio, in which there is a small fountain surrounded by roman statues and capitals.

The Archaeological Museum is one of the most important of its type in Spain. Among the numerous collection of pieces which it owns, are the famous bronze stag, discovered in the arab ruins of Medina Azahara, and the stone lion, which comes from Nueva Carteya, together they powerfully call ones attention.

There are numerous and interesting objects that one can see in the different rooms, and among them we must mention the Neanderthalic fossil remains, pieces from the Neolithic period, and sculptures of totem-like animals from the Bronze Age, throwing darts, and the bronze sacrificial bulls found in the iberic sanctuaries of the Collado in the gardens of Jaén...

The sculptures are also really wonderful, among those which stand out are the bust of the emperor Commodo, and a head of Germanico, also the roman and arab mosaics, and in the same manner an artistic paleochristian sarcophagus.

The archaeological collection of the museum is really impressive; from the neolithic remains found in the marshland of the Guadalmellato, to the mudejar traces; coins, jewels, ceramics, coffers, passing by the works of the ceramics, the roman lead sarcophagi, a precious bronze arab brazier, the wonderful collection of arabian and mudejar well curbstones, or the visigothic crosses from the treasury of Torredonjimeno.

The excavations that are being carried out have already realized pleasing results in the unmasking of important roman ruins.

A magnificent body of an Iberic lion, found in Nueva Carteya, it forms part of the valuable estate of the Archaelogical Museum of Cordova.

An artistic mosaic of the Valenzoleja that is exhibited in one of the rooms of the Archaelogical Museum.

An artistic Christian tomb on show in the Archaelogical Museum of Cordova.

MUSEO HISTORICO DE LA CIUDAD

It is installed in the castle of Calahorra, an Arabian fortress, possibly of the XIV century, on the site of which there was previously a Roman fortress. The Calahorra experienced, after the conquest of Cordova by the Christian troops, some modifications and was profoundly restored in the XV century. The word Calahorra comes it seems, from *Calat,* that means castle, and *Horr,* that means open space. So, Calahorra would mean *Castillo libre* (airy castle) or something similar.

The tower of the Calahorra, its solid silhouette uplifted at the side of the Guadalquivir, at one of the ends of the Roman Bridge.

The castle of the Calahorra and the tower of the Malmuerta, the construction of which, at the beginning of the XV century, was imposed by Enrique III on a gentleman that killed his wife impulsed by groundless jealousy, are two of the most characteristic monuments of Cordova. La Calahorra is found to the extreme south of the Roman bridge.

It is a solid construction, of one storey in the shape of a cross with embattled fortified towers. On the other side of the bridge are found the old ruins of the windmill of Albolafia.

A statue of San Fernando, carved in wood, that can be found in the Historical Museum of the city, installed in the Calahorra.

In the room of the Historical Museum dedicated to Góngora, written on wood, is this famous sonnet "A Córdoba" (To Cordova), at the side of the head of the great Cordovan poet.

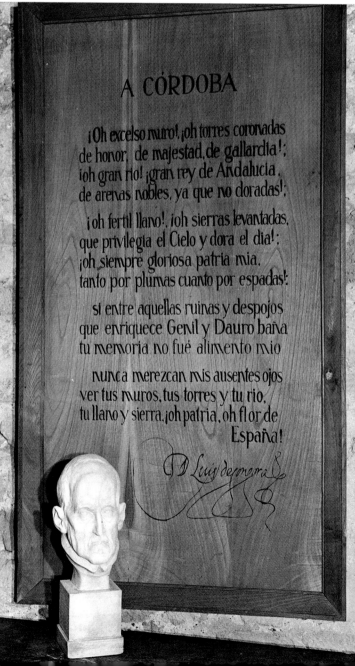

A CÓRDOBA

¡Oh excelso muro!, ¡oh torres coronadas
de honor, de majestad, de gallardía!;
¡oh gran río! ¡gran rey de Andalucía,
de arenas nobles, ya que no doradas!;

¡oh fértil llano!, ¡oh sierras levantadas,
que privilegia el Cielo y dora el día!;
¡oh siempre gloriosa patria mía,
tanto por plumas cuanto por espadas!:

si entre aquellas ruinas y despojos
que enriquece Genil y Dauro baña
tu memoria no fué alimento mío

nunca merezcan mis ausentes ojos
ver tus muros, tus torres y tu río,
tu llano y sierra, ¡oh patria, oh flor de
España!

D. Luis de Góngora

Today the Calahorra houses the interesting Historical Museum of the city, and inside its bright rooms, that seem even more animated by the breath of their illustrious past, are kept interesting Royal Charters allusive to Cordova, and a valuable collection of works of art and antiques. There are two busts of the Gran Capitán, one carved by Ruiz de Olmos and the other, by Mateo Inurria, and a curious wooden carving of Fernando III el Santo.

Of particular interest is the so-called Sala de Tapices the intelligent arrangement of which allows it to keep the medieval profile of the room and excites spiritual remembrances. There is also a room dedicated to Góngora, the great Cordova poet of the Golden Century of Spanish literature, in which is kept a bust of the author of *Polifemo* at the side of a magnificent sonnet, written on a tablet, that has the title "A Córdoba". In the foreground the Guadalquivir, ample and majestic, and the ruins of four ancient Arabian windmills.

Looking towards the country-side that extends in front of the city, on the other side of the Guadalquivir, one begins to be insensibly absorbed, and Cordova with its agitated and noble historical past, with its spiritual personality, with everything, when summing up that which represents Cordova artistically and literary, takes hold of the town.

An aspect of the magnificent Sala de Tapices of the Historical Museum of the city.

An artistic set of silver used by the Cabildo to collect votes. It can be seen in the Museo Municipal de Arte Cordobés and Taurino

The front of the embossed silver altar of the oratory of the Casas Consistoriales (Town Hall).

MUSEO MUNICIPAL DE ARTE CORDOBES Y TAURINO

Housed in the Plaza de Maimónides one enters the museum through a patio. On the ground floor one can admire a collection of goat skins and several Arabian chairs of embossed leather; also other objects of great interest, among those of note is a set of silver-salver that was used for the votes of the municipal Chapter house, of the Casas Consistoriales, work of the Cordova silversmith, XVI century, Juan Sánchez.

A magnificent goatskin belonging to the collection of embossed skins that can be admired in the Municipal Museum.

In a small room you can contemplate the office of Lagartijo el Grande, exactly as it was in his house in the Calle Osorio.

In another room there is a bust of "El Cordobés" and at the side of it the suit of lights used by him the day of his admission as matador. After this room is a room dedicated to Manolete, one of the most eminent bullfighting figures of the school of Cordova. You can contemplate a bust of this great bull-fighter painted by Vázquez Díaz. His lying down statue, on the tomb of the bullfighter, work of Ruiz Olmos, and various pictures and photographs, such as that of the cape, the red cloth, the sword and the stick that Manolete used in his last bullfight, which cost him his life in Linares.

An aspect of the office of Lagartijo el Grande, which occupies a room in the Museo Taurino of Cordova

One of the curious ancient posters of the collection of the Museo Taurino of Cordova (Bullfighting Museum of Cordova).

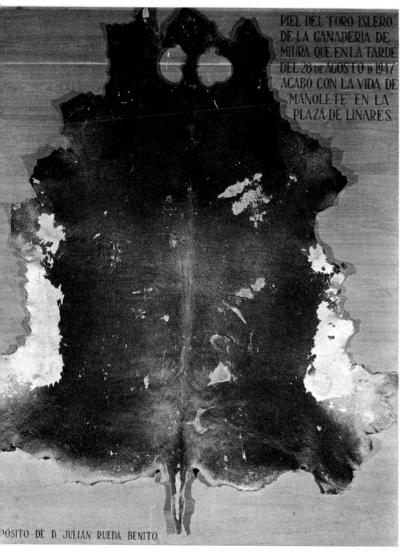

Skin of "Islero", the bull that killed Manolete, which is kept in the Museo Taurino of Cordova.

The cape used by Manolete in the Plaza de Toros of Linares, the day of his death.

The tomb of Manolete, in white marble, which is found in the cemetery of Nuestra Señora de la Salud.

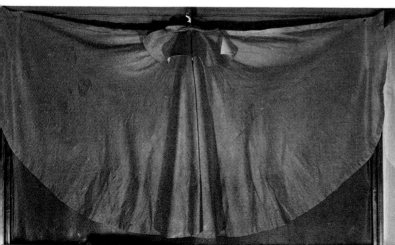

The façade of the new bull ring of Cordova, of an agile modern outline.

CORDOVA AND THE BULLS

The people of Cordova form with those of Seville and Ronda, the great trio of bullfighting schools of Andalusia. The so called National fiesta is profoundly enrooted in Cordova. The Tienta, a picturesque field fiesta in which the braveness of the young bulls is tried out, constitutes a powerfully attractive folkloric scene of the lands of Cordova. Among the long list of noble bullfighters that Cordova has produced must be noted Pepete I, Cúchares, Bocanegra, Lagartijo el Grande, Guerrita, Manolete and el Cordobés.

THE "DIPUTACION PROVINCIAL"

This occupies the ancient building of the convent of La Merced. It has various patios, among those which stand out most is the one at the entrance, with wide arches and a fountain in the middle, and another of Renaissance style. The church is Baroque, with a Churrigueresque porch, and inside you can admire several interesting sculptures.

In the Palace of the Deputation, the town hall is provisionally housed, because on the sight of its own building in the calle Claudio Marcelo some important Roman remains were found.

The façade of the Palace of the Diputación Provincial (Provincial Deputation) ancient convent of the Mercedarios, housed in the Plaza de Colón.

FOLKLORE OF CORDOVA

Cordova has been considered as "the capital of the big songs". The people of Cordova do not sing in chorus but individually. They only need the accompaniment of the guitar to make the most profound melodies of the "cante jondo" flow from their chests. It has already been said by García Lorca, in these beautiful precious verses:

Cuando yo me muera
enterradme con mi guitarra
bajo la arena.

The fandango is made up of five verses; it extends itself over the lands of Cordova through three different paths: that of Cordova, that of the Cabra, and that of the Lucena. The three however come from the same lyrical branch, anciently centred in the "Cordova far away and alone", the centre of an accused cultural and artistic focus point, of an open personality.

The three facets of the songs of Cordova, in order to differentiate them, are known by the names of "Alegría de Córdoba", the "soleá" and the "serrana". While the first had it seems, its origin in the marches of Cádiz, and later acquired its birthright in Cordova, the "serrana" is the popular expression of the countryside, full of romance and also certain pastoral traces.

The Plaza de la Corredera, with its unmistakable popular air, its picturesque variation, with its stalls in the open air in the centre and its bars and taverns under the porches, constitutes a lively folkloric picture of the typical atmosphere of Cordova.

The "soleá" is perhaps the most genuine expression of the lyrics of Cordova, the voice of the singer sinks into him in order to let out, bit by bit, all the effect of the feeling that grips him. The full-blooded Cordovan singer suffers, but restrains his wantoness and whispers with elegance the "soleá", this gift of the singer of Cordova that the popular genius of García Lorca knew how to capture and transfer to these verses of substancial fidelity:

> *Vestida con mantos negros*
> *piensa que el mundo es chiquito*
> *y el corazón es inmenso.*
> *Piensa que el suspiro tierno*
> *y el grito desaparecen*
> *en la corriente del viento.*
> *Se dejó el balcón abierto*
> *y al alba por el balcón*
> *desembocó todo el cielo.*
> *¡Ay yayayayay,*
> *que vestida con mantos negros!*

The "soleá" and the "vito" are the two dances of Cordova for their excellence. The first is danced to the accompaniment of the guitar and a voice singing the "soleá".

The "vito" is danced to the accompaniment of the accordian around a central point. The "bailadoras" (dancers) dance with the big black hats of Cordova and wear flashy shawls.

A leather-worker working a skin, a traditional facet of the craftsmanship of Cordova.

Silver has always found in Cordova clever craftsmen who worked it and decorated it with art and love...

The presence of the Cordovan rider and the nervous elegance of the arab horse makes a beautiful picture of marked character.

Among the different folkloric manifestations that are celebrated in Cordova, standing out because of their accused soft and human profilé, is the already mentioned Festival of the patios of Cordova, the May fair and the Autumn fair. The first begins on the 25th. May, and lasts until the beginning of June. During these days are celebrated important bull-fights, classical theatrical works, and pieces of opera. The streets of the city are invaded by a picturesque cluster of tents, inside which are sold pieces of ceramic, objects of filigreed silver, embossed leather and other objects of the traditional crafts of Cordova.

A handsome group of young Cordovans, wearing typical costumes, walking through the streets in the middle of the May festival.

During the May fair and also in the Autumn one, the latter being much less animated and spectacular, one can admire the dexterity with which the brave horsemen of Cordova ride through the streets of the city, alone or carrying behind them this marvellous dark flower of flesh which is the woman of Cordova.

The song is born in Cordova as are the wines of Moriles and of Montilla, together, they are elements of the typical atmosphere.

A magnificent picture of two fighting bulls free to roam at will.

A gallant Cordovan rider carrying behind him a splendid dark woman.

THE GASTRONOMY OF CORDOVA

As a general rule, above all in the ancient part of the city, the taverns of Cordova keep, fortunately intact, their typical intimacy. They are normally quiet places, nooks, where you can eat and drink with a certain philosophical air, as Seneca?, without any traces of bad taste.

The people of Cordova taste their wine with elegant sensuality. White wines from Montilla and from Moriles, golden aromatic wines of exquisite *bouquet,* an ideal bond between the senses and the spirit served in the slender wine tubes, directly poured from the barrel. The limpidness of the wine which is drunk in Cordova, its aroma and its flavour, possibly also have something to say at the time of inventing the influences that mould the balanced character of the people of Cordova. However, such dishes of forceful personality cannot go unmentioned, as for example, the stew made with the tail of the bull, the dish with frogs cooked in tomato, the lamb, caldereta style or the spicy snails. Neither can one forget the white gazpacho soup, deliciously refreshing. In respect to the chapter about desserts, one must take into account the Cordovan cake, the polvorones and the orange "miga".

The stew of the tail of the bull is one of the most popular dishes on the Cordovan menu.

Among the typical Cordovan desserts, the pastelon occupies a place of honour.

MEDINA AZAHARA

At some eight kilometres from Cordova, on the western part of the Sierra, there is, like a symbol of a noble Moslem past, the beautiful ruins of Medina Azahara. The city, considered as the Arabian Versailles, was constructed by Abderraman III in the X century, and was enlarged and beautified by his successors, until, at the beginning of the XI century it was plundered by the Berbers. The construction of Medina Azahara lasted twenty five years and its existence did not last more than seventy four years.

The ruins of this beautiful Arabian patio seem to still guard the memory of the splendour of Medina Azahara.

The history of Medina Azahara is surrounded by a popular air of romance. It seems, at least according to its popular legend, that Abderraman III constructed the enchanting city in honour of the beautiful Zahara, his favourite wife

Medina Azahara was, according to all indications, the reigning capital during its brief period of existence, that is to say, palace and court of the caliphs. It was populated by some twelve thousand inhabitants, and in its precinct housed important branches of the administration of the Arabian state.

Today, its ruins can be seen impregnated with melancholy, inside the protection of the pine trees that face it along the side of the Sierra, surrounded by olive trees and evergreens.

Near to Medina Azahara, at some six kilometres from Cordova one can find the ruins of the Alamiriya, a small city constructed by Almanzor.

Today, it is nothing more than a landmark, beaten and eaten away by time, which however, permits the evocation of the historical greatness of the Caliphate of Cordova.

Medina Azahara was a city whose structure was made of terraced like steps that were adapted

The reconstruction of this room of one of the sumptuous Arabian palaces that is found in Medina Azahara allows one to imagine the magnificence, today beaten and in ruins, of that city constructed in the X century a few kilometres from Cordova.

An aspect of the ruins of Medina Azahara, whose melancholy seems to be projected by the tall presence of the cypress trees.

The filigreed work which can still be appreciated in some of the remains is evidence of a high artistic sense of the architects that built Medina Azahara.

An artistical base and a marvellous capital found among the ruins of Medina Azahara.

to the unevenness of the Sierra, separated one from the other by great walls. The palaces occupied the highest part of the city. Then came the urban zone of the centre, gardens and allotments, green spaces that separated the court from the lower part of the city, where in its turn, the large mosque was found, and the houses inhabited by the more humble people.

The ruins offer a reflection of the sumptuousness of Medica Azahara in its splendid years. Eveything must have been magnificent and beautiful in the precinct of that Mohammedan town, judging by the magnificence and artistic grace that can still be seen decking the remains of the white marble capitals, the paintings, socles, foundations, aqueducts and columns.

THE ARRUZAFA

To the left of the old path to the Ermitas you find the Parador de Turismo of the Arruzafa, the building of which has been constructed on the same site where before there was a small palace of recreation of Abderraman I.

The Parador is splendidly situated, dominating a beautiful wide panoramic view, with Cordova in the background. It is surrounded by pretty gardens invaded by flowers, the happy colours of which extend, jubilantly and freely under the poetic shade of some tall palm trees.

The façade of the Parador (hotel) Nacional de la Arruzafa, from where you can get a wide and beautiful panoramic view.

The presence of the University Laboral "Onésimo Redondo" on the outskirts of the city shows that Cordova has not gone to sleep on the laurels of the past.

An aspect of the ultra modern instalations of the University Laboral of Cordova.

THE ERMITAS

Situated in the middle of the Sierra, with quite a distance between them, they can be sighted from Cordova. The actual Sanctuaries are at some fifteen kilometres from the city, in the same places that they occupied long ago, installed there in the first days of christianity and whose existence was respected during the Arabian rule. The wild pair are crowned by a church of the XVIII century and by a monument to the Sagrado Corazón erected in 1929. From the Sanctuaries you can get an extensive and beautiful panoramic view.

The entrance to the church that crowns the small hill where the Sanctuaries are, looks like the picture of a romantic engraving.

From the natural magnificent look out of the Sanctuaries one can contemplate the city of Cordova rising over the countryside fertilized by the Guadalquivir.

CORDOVA BY NIGHT

To go round the city under the moonlight makes up a merry and unforgettable spiritual adventure, of surprising and singular sensual aesthetic scenes.

If one goes along the beautiful Calleja de las Flores through the Plaza de los Dolores, the last resting place of silence, through the calle of San Fernando, a living apotheosis of oranges, or if you go down to the edge of the Guadalquivir, one gets the impression of living in a magic world, where all beauty has its place...

History seems to ride crazily through the Cordovan night, to the most penetrating corners of the city. And so, on arriving at the calle Cabeza and entering through a narrow and small lane, we imagine the bloody heads of the seven infants of Lara hanging from the seven stone arches that join one wall to the other.

Or we imagine a human figure crossing under the pale light of the old street lamp, that is the very Don Luis de Góngora y Argote, who, as said in the verses of Luis Cernuda:

Harto de los años tan largos malgas-
tados
En perseguir fortuna lejos de Córdoba
la llana y de su muro excelso
Vuelve al rincón nativo para morir
tranquilo y silencioso...

Cordova, "Romana o mora"
(Roman or Moorish) as Machado
said, open at dusk the great wings
of your spirit completely and drown
the atmosphere in the mystery of
your personal bewitching.

Index

Putting this volume in your hands the desire of the Editor is to bring to your mind the most intimate and profound essence of a fragment of that varied and always palpitating ancient part of history that is "The bull's skin" (The shape that Spain takes on the map) of Spain. For this, has been used the vehicle of a Kaleidoscopic succession of spectacular photographic images. If he has achieved his desire, the Editor will feel extremely satisfied as that, with it, he will have helped give a larger and better knowledge of Spain.

Other titles of the collection ALL SPAIN

The printing of this book was completed
in the workshops of FISA - Industrias
Gráficas, Palaudarias, 26 - Barcelona
(Spain)